Looking for Potholes

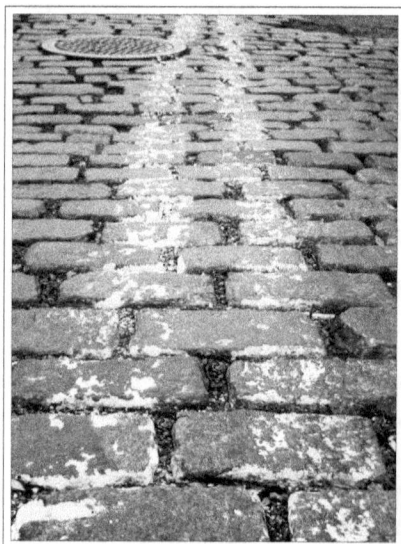

Joe Wenke

Looking for Potholes

Poems

trans
über

Stamford, Connecticut   2015

For Mark, Ryan, Olivia and Gisele

Contents

I Don't Have to Be Right 1

Running Out 2

Then and Now 3

Looking for Potholes 4

Lying Liars 5

Simple Question 6

Happy Day 8

Withdrawal 10

Time Bomb 11

Dog 12

The Puppet 13

The Waiter 14

End Times 15

Spooky 17

At the Strip Club 19

Yes Man 20

Back Talk 21

The Game 23

Regrets 24

Counting 25

Swerve 26

Declaration of Independence 27

I Walk Around 28

The Boot 29

Know It All 30

Touché 31

Trouble 32

The Stranger 33

Odd Couple 34

Choosy 36

Ready 38

Homage 39

Done 40

Insignificant Other 41

The Holy Family 42

Pretty Please 43

Maniac 44

The Tin Man 45

The Geater with the Heater 46

Stand Up 47

Up the Booty Hole 48

My Prayer 49

Late Bloomer 51

Silence, Please 52

No 53

Over 54

Trapped 55

Floating 56

Some Day 57

A Place 58

Looking for Potholes

I Don't Have to Be Right

I don't have to be right.
Wrong is fine with me.
I'm used to it.
At this point
I just want to
let it be.

Who was right?
Who was wrong?
Who remembers?

I used to know you so well,
and now you're gone.

What's left?

What I could have said.
What I could have done.

Would saying or doing
something different
have made a difference?
Maybe it would,
but I could be wrong.

Running Out

I'm not going to run
out of ideas.
I'm just going to run
out of time.
There is no end
to my ideas,
but there is an end
to me
and to you and you
and you and you
and you.
All of you
sooner or later
whatever you do
or don't do,
whatever you know
or don't know.
That's my idea.
That's it.
That's one more
in the run
with no end in sight
until I'm done.

Then and Now

I used to drink soda.
Now I don't.
You used to make small talk.
Now you won't.

I used to shoot baskets.
Now I'm shot.
You used to be with me.
Now you're not.

I used to flip houses.
Now they flop.
You used to keep going.
Now you stop.

We're here for the moment.
No one knows
how long you stay open,
when you close.

Looking for Potholes

I'm driving real fast
on this dark
and creepy road,
driving real fast
and looking for potholes,
looking for the bumps
in the road,
looking for the hairpin turns
and the narrow escapes,
driving like I mean it,
driving with a mission,
out on my own,
looking to arrive
a little out of whack,
a little bit twisted,
a little worse for wear
with an axe to grind
and an attitude
to share,
tearing up the streets
like nobody else but me.

Lying Liars

Lie just to keep in practice.
No matter what the fact is,
they lie
because they like to.
They need to.
It's their
reason for being.
It's their style.
It makes life worthwhile
for them
to lie
about this, that
and the other,
about everything
and nothing.
They lie
to your face,
and they lie
behind your back.
Distort,
deceive,
because they think
that everyone believes
the filth
that comes out
of their mouths.

Simple Question

You seem so nice.
You have such a quiet voice.
It's so soothing and sweet.
You sound like a psychologist
or a priest.
Actually now that I think of it,
you sound a lot
like my urologist
just before he checks
my prostate.

By all appearances
you are trustworthy and true,
kind, considerate, sincere —
almost impossibly chill.
In fact, you demonstrate
such skill
in all your
interpersonal affairs,
I might even consider
making you the executor
of my will.

Unfortunately,
there's just
one small issue here.
You see
I've been informed

by more than one
reliable source
that behind my back
you attack me.
You trash me
to everyone you meet.
Basically, you assassinate my character
every chance you get.

Now that just doesn't seem to fit
with the nice quiet voice,
the soothing and sweet,
the trustworthy and true,
the kind, the considerate,
the sincere and the chill.

So what am I to think?
What am I to do?
You tell me.
No better yet,
how about answering
this one simple question?
Exactly who the hell are you?

Happy Day

I'm so happy,
so full of joy
and positive energy.
I woke up this way
this morning.
I wish I knew why.

Was it what she said
to me in her text
right before I went to bed?

Or maybe a dream I had?
I know there was a good one,
but I forget what it was.

Could it even be
the simple fact
that I'm alive
and breathing?
Is that the reason
I'm so happy today?

I don't know.
It's just so unlike me
to wake up this way.
It bugs me
that I don't know why.

Then again
maybe I should just
kick back
and accept it
as a lucky break,
claim it as a gift,
set the timer
on my **iPhone**
and see how
long it takes
before it lifts.

Withdrawal

I sit in my chair
and stare into space.
I barely show my face
anywhere.
There is hardly
a trace of me left
in the world.

Nevertheless,
I still get the same bills.
I still take the same pills.
The haters keep hating.
The takers keep taking.
The fakers keep faking.

Apparently,
though I've stopped engaging,
except for the aging,
the war keeps on waging.
No one's noticed I'm gone.

Time Bomb

I'm going to blow.
I don't know when.
I just know
I will.
I could go off with anybody,
family, friends, strangers.
I could be in a crowd.
I could go off alone.

The last time
was so bad.
I just snapped.
I tried to stop,
but once it started,
there was no going back.

I get scared,
so I run.
They catch me.
I hit the ground,
and I'm done.

I wish I could just go
somewhere,
go someplace,
where I didn't have to be me.

But there is no place
for me to go,
and so I know
that it will happen.
I just don't know when
I'll blow.

Dog

Don't bark at me, dog!
That's a bad doggy.
Of course,
you're not a dog.
You're a human being,
and it's not becoming
as a human being
to act like a beast,
to bark like a dog,
to growl
and show your teeth,
your dirty yellow teeth.

Oh, you didn't know that?
Well, you know it now,
dog.

Don't bark at me!

The Puppet

She's the puppeteer,
and you're the puppet.
You look miserable,
but I think you love it.
It's who you are.
It's all you'll ever be,
her puppet.

The Waiter

I'm a great waiter,
not of food
but for what is to come,
waiting for love,
waiting for loss,
waiting for what comes
and what goes,
waiting for the inevitable flow
of life
to wash over me
as it did yesterday
and as it does today.

End Times

With apologies to Barbara Lewis

I'm really not one
to get too concerned
about much of anything.

But last night around ten
the stars fell from the sky,
at least the ones
over my house,
and early this morning
I learned
that our well had run dry.

Then just a few minutes ago,
my good friend,
Farmer Jones,
was on the phone
telling me
his cows had come home.

Now ordinarily
I would think that,
however odd,
these separate incidents
were all mere
coincidence,
but here's what worries me
a smidge.
I just checked
the fridge,

and I'm almost
out of rhymes.

You heard me right.
There are just a few,
and then I'm through.

So may I admit
before I quit
that I must self-indict.
I once was deceived,
but now I believe.
Good God,
we must be in
End Times!

Spooky

If there's one thing I know,
it's this:
on you I can depend.

Whenever I'm alone,
getting a little too deeply
ensconced
in my personal comfort zone,
you magically
appear
like a specter
or a bone collector,
like a ghost.

You creep me out.
You make my blood
run cold.
You make my hair
stand up.
You possess my mind
and inhabit
my soul.
You haunt my house.

Yes, you!
With your perfectly timed
reminders
of disaster and destruction,
of mortality and loss
and how it all will end,

you're my imaginary creature,
my personal kabuki,
the freakiest of reapers
and the sleepiest of sleepers.

You're my dearest,
best friend,
Spooky!

At the Strip Club

Broke ass motherfuckers
up against the wall,
eyeing every bitch.
They wanna have a ball.
They wanna scratch their itch,
but they got no scratch,
no fish for the fish,
no jingle for the juice,
no paper for the pussy,
no bone for the booty,
no cheddar for the cheese,
no cash for the cutie,
no bank for the yank,
no bling for the thing,
no chips for the hole,
no wad in the wallet,
no ducats in the pocket,
no rocket in the socket,
no coin for the boing,
no wang for the tang.
Yeah, their heads are gonna hang.
You know they gotta blow
cos they got no bang.
They got no dough.

Yes Man

Yes, ma'am.
Yes, sir.
Ok.
Whatever you say.
You got it.
Your way.
Agreed.
Guaranteed.
Whatever you need.
I'll hop to it.
Glad to do it.
No trouble.
On the double.
My pleasure.
Without measure.
For goodness sakes.
Whatever it takes.
I'm your man.
That's the plan.
No mistakes.
No faux pas.
That's because
you are the boss.

Back Talk

Cut me some slack,
babe!
I mean
back off just a bit.
You're in my face, hon,
and I don't like it.
You get
a little too
up close
and personal
for my personal taste,
Attila,
just a wee bit too
testicular.
In fact,
a little tact
and restraint
wouldn't kill you.
You're way too goddamn
demanding
for my money,
and you're just wasting
your time
if you think
your particular brand
of jive
flies with me.

To be perfectly blunt,
you're obnoxious, sweetie.

Actually,
"bitch" and "cunt"
are two words
that come to mind,
though I refrain
from using them
out of respect
for your kind.

In future
unless and until
your manners refine
may I suggest
a simple solution:
You go your way.
I go mine.

The Game

It's a simple game
to play
with two simple rules:

No. 1:
I'm always right.

No. 2:
You're always wrong.

To wit:
Whenever you say "yes,"
the correct answer is "no."

When you say "no,"
well, we both know
how that goes.

Questions?

Then let's play!

Regrets

Fuck Frank Sinatra!
I regret
everything I've ever done.
Every decision
I've ever made,
every single one,
was wrong.
But I can't go back,
so I'm on the attack.
Get out of my way.
Today is the day.
I start over.

Counting

I'm counting on you
to be the one.
I had thought
there was none.
I'm counting on you
to stay,
to be true.
You need to be you.
I need to be me,
but we are
best together.
You are the bravest person
I know.
Be brave for us both.
I'm counting on you,
I hope,
forever.

Swerve

I swerve on the curve,
but I keep my nerve.
I hop on the ledge.
I dance on the edge
of existence.
I move through the dark,
doing the math,
taking the path
of greatest resistance,
knowing the odds,
ignoring the gods.
What I do
is none
of their business.

Declaration of Independence

I'm knocking things out,
removing all doubt.
I'm wiping the floor,
and I'm asking for more.

I'm drawing a crowd.
I'm getting it loud,
the oohs and the ahs
and the cool lah-di-dahs.

I'm shooting the moon.
I'm calling the tune.
I'm ringing the bell,
and I'm raising some hell.

You hate me?
You love me?
That's your deal.
I don't care
what you think.

I'm just keeping it real.

I Walk Around

I walk around
with my pants falling down.
Some people don't like it.
They get a bit emotional,
but I don't care.
Let them stare.
After all
it's just a little ass crack,
and it makes me feel
like I got something going on
down there.

The Boot

I got the boot
last night.
We're having a fight,
and I start
to shoot
my mouth off
like I'm so smart
or something,
like she's good
for nothing,
and I'm the one
who's right
about whatever it is
that went wrong.
I can't remember
what it was
right now
or how
any of it happened,
but does
that even matter
at this point?
I mean
this is not
what I had planned.
Maybe I should
make a visit.
Then again
exactly what part
of get the fuck out
of here is it
that I don't understand?

Know It All

I know what you want me to say,
but I'm not going to say it.
This time
I won't give you that satisfaction.
Our interactions are always
so predictable and polite.
Let's mix it up a bit.
I'm tired
of the same old same old shit.
We're way too nice to each other.
How about we have a little fight,
a little disagreement?
It would do us some good.
Put a little spice
in the relationship.
Kick up a little dirt.
What do you say?
Hey! What was that?
I didn't say hit me, hon.
You know, that hurt!

Touché

You say
I'm too aggressive,
too obsessive,
too impressed with myself.

Too picky,
too boozy,
too wacky,
too choosy.

It's always "too"
with you.

What would you say
if you woke up
one day,
and I was
just right for you?

Trouble

You look like trouble,
the way you walk,
the way you talk.
I think I like that.
I've been around trouble before.
It turns into a mess
every time,
but I don't care.
How about a drink?
We can take it from there.

The Stranger

Last night
we saw each other
for the first time
in years.
My fears
of an epic confrontation,
an ugly conflagration
sparked by a chance encounter —
the accidental meeting
of two people
who once loved
but then profoundly
hated each other —
were unfounded.
You looked at me
for just a moment
with no change in expression
or sign of recognition
that I could see.
Then you turned away
from me
and walked on —
as if you were
a total stranger.

Odd Couple

Not that I care,
of course.
Call it curiosity,
but one day
it will all be clear
to me.

I'll puzzle out the clues.
I'll see through the ruse —
all your claptrap
about children
and family,
about fidelity
and faith,
all your phony baloney
posturing and posing.
You know —
the super mom in action,
the quiet doting dad,
the carefully crafted facade
that strikes everyone as odd
and oh so painfully sad.

Some day
I'll crack the code.
I'll tap
into the mother lode,

the stark reality
of your pact
of self-delusion
and despair.

Then I'll know
the ugly truth.
I'll know the facts
behind the lies.
I'll know the real reason why
you two are a pair.

Choosy

You say I'm too choosy,
but I chose you,
right?
Why are you so uptight?
That's worse than being
choosy.

I'm just particular.
What's wrong with that?
It means I've got taste.
I know what's what,
what's in,
what's out,
what's over, hon.
It's about selectivity
and style.
Sorry if you find it
off-putting
or nasty.
Would you prefer
that I waste my time
on trash?
If I lash out
against mediocrity,
against what's crass
and second rate,
it's because I care.
A perfectionist?

Yeah! That's me,
but that's good,
not bad.
It means I stand
for something.
I don't defer
to others
just to get along.
It's called integrity,
and if that makes me
a pain in the ass,
so be it.

Ready

I can't wait forever.
I'm part
of the space-time continuum,
living within the curvature of space,
the arc of mortality.
I can't wait forever
for you.
If you are waiting for me,
I'm ready,
ready for you,
ready for anything
together.
The time is now.
Let's get on
with the adventure.

Homage

You are spectacular!
You are!
May I blow your horn?

You've got the vigor
and the verve,
the swagger and the swerve.
You got the dagger of my dreams
and those magical curves.
You got those titular motions
that cause the commotion,
that make me unload
in an ocean of lotion,
make me bust my seams,
make my throat start to sing,
put my mind in a trance,
make me drive off the road.
Yes, you know how to bring
that ring a ding ding
to my pants.

What more can I say?
You know how to sway.
You show me the way,
and I worship the day
you were born.
Spectacular!

Done

I'm done
with you.
There's nothing more
I can do.
I'm through
being tolerant
and kind.
I'm through
with the hope,
trying to find
a way to make it work.
I'm done
trying to understand,
trying to start over again,
knowing what I know,
when what I know is this:
It's time for me to go.

Insignificant Other

We have a binding contract
to which we scrupulously adhere
and ratify without revision
on the first of each year.

Though quite involved
the essentials are as follows:
Never talk.
Never share.
Never true.
Never care.
Never trust.
Never there.

Always father.
Always mother.
Ever and always,
the insignificant other.

The Holy Family

How did you get
that halo
on your head?
And not just you,
your whole family too?
I mean it.
What's your secret?
How did it appear?
I've been trying
to get that special effect
for years.
Is it because you're so good and holy,
not to mention rich?
You're a pompous ass.
Your wife's a fucking bitch,
and your kids are brats,
but you've all got
that little lit up hat
on your heads.
Oh, that's it?
You say
it comes
with the yacht club membership.
Why didn't I think of that?

Pretty Please

I want to
touch touch touch it
so much much much it
is giving me pain
like a sprain in my brain,
like a shock to my clock,
like a burn on my yearn,
like a knock to my knees,
like a cry in my eyes.

It's making me squirm,
making me wriggle
and writhe
and slither
and slide.
It's making me churn,
this burn on my yearn.
It's getting to me
with the cry in my eyes
and the knock to my knees
and the shock to my clock
and the sprain in my brain.

So may I explain
that this terrible pain
will greatly be eased
if I may pretty please
just touch touch touch it.

Maniac

I'm a maniac.
Hop on my back,
and we'll ride
until we wreck,
tailgating fate,
running up
the ass of existence.

The Tin Man

Mitt Romney's got nothing on you.
In fact, you could teach him
a thing or two —
pedantic,
robotic
and oh so weirdly neurotic,
your sociability premeditated
and professionally medicated,
deliberately late,
making everybody wait,
withholding information —
it's a powerful combination
with just one tiny little issue:
You never can be trusted.
One day you'll turn up rusted —
the Tin Man.
That's you.

The Geater with the Heater

If you see a line,
cross it.
If you have the ball,
toss it.
If you hold the string,
floss it.
If you got the goods,
go.

Don't ask for permissions
or formal commissions.
Don't wait for instructions
or fancy productions.

If you are the leader,
the Geater with the Heater,
you cross it.
You toss it.
You floss it
and go.

Stand Up

You pay every day
for being who you are
one way
or the other.
You can lose
family and friends.
It can mean the end
of cherished relationships.
You can suffer abuse.
You can be accused
of everything you're not,
but the payback is huge.
You choose
to be free.
You choose
to stand up
for equality.
You choose
love and peace,
while the haters hate
and the others wait.
You make the difference.
You create new ways
of being
for yourself
and everyone.

Up the Booty Hole

I want you to go
up the booty hole.
I want to know.
Is that where my soul
is?
Is that
where it's happening?
Is that
where it's at?
I'm on a roll.
I'm on the stroll,
and I think
this is the time
to commit the crime
of being
who I am.

My Prayer

Dear Devil,
please make me thinner.
If you do,
I promise I'll become
the world's greatest sinner.
I'm pretty bad already,
but I know
I can do better.
I'll do anything to be thin:
Lie, cheat, steal,
slander, gossip —
you can check all those boxes.
Anything sexy,
I'm down with that.
I'll masturbate, fornicate,
sodomize too.
Take my love to town?
You got it!
Done!

Oh, Serpent, most powerful,
I am proud to be your shill.
What the hell, I'll even kill
for you.
I'll provide you
with a whole list of candidates,
people I hate.
You just tell me who.

In conclusion,
if there is anything I missed,

by all means just
add it to the list.

And so, my dearest Devil,
My Lucifer,
My Lord,
please hear me when I pray.
I shall do absolutely
anything for you
if you will make me thin today.

Late Bloomer

There's less time
all the time.
There's no time
to lose.
I'm a late bloomer,
baby boomer,
late to the party,
slow to arrive.
I need to move faster
to escape the disaster
that looms.

Silence, Please

Shut your mouth.
Don't speak.
I know what's going
through your head.
I know the hate
that pulses through your veins.
Don't pretend.
You're not my friend.
I know what you want.
You want me dead.
I see it in your eyes
and in your smile.
I feel it in the way
you shake my hand.
So shut your mouth.
Don't speak.
I get the message,
not the one that's in your mouth,
the one that's in your head.

No

No black
No say
No brown
No way
No trans
No gay
No free
Nowhere
No voice
No care
No chance
No break
No give
No take
No hope
No see
No you
No me.

Over

It happens
on its own.
You don't decide
when it's over.
Once you know,
it's done.
What you had
is gone for good.
It doesn't matter
what you feel.
It doesn't matter
what you do.
It will never
be the same.
You can never
go back.
You can never recover
what's lost.
You've reached
the end,
and there's no
starting over.

Trapped

I'm trapped inside.
I can't get out.
My hands are tied.
My nose is closed.
My eyes are glued.
My mouth is gagged.
My ears are plugged.

There is no air.
I don't know where
I am. My brain
is shutting down.
I know nothing.

But the darkness
is dark and deep.
I want to sleep,
but I'm awake.
I cannot take
this existence.

Floating

I'm floating
in the middle
of the ocean,
floating along
easy and free.
I could swim
this way
or that,
but why?
What would that
get me?
Better to continue
floating.
Better to conserve
my energy
until the *deus ex machina*
arrives
with some suntan lotion
and a one-way ticket
to paradise.

Some Day

Some day
I'll be in a museum.
Sorry,
I meant mausoleum
or in an urn
on somebody's mantle
or maybe in their garage
next to the paint thinner
when it's my turn
to go.

A Place

I'm looking
for a place
to be,
a place to rest.
I'm looking
for the best place
for me
to spend
my remaining time
on this planet.
Where is this place
for me?
What place is best?
Is it here
or there?
Is it anywhere?
Is there a place
for me
that's best?

JOE WENKE is a writer, social critic and LGBTQ rights activist. He is the founder and publisher of Trans Über, a publishing company with a focus on promoting LGBTQ rights, free thought and equality for all people. Wenke received a B.A. in English from the University of Notre Dame, an M.A. in English from Penn State and a Ph.D. in English from the University of Connecticut.

Author's photo by Gisele Alicea (aka Gisele Xtravaganza)

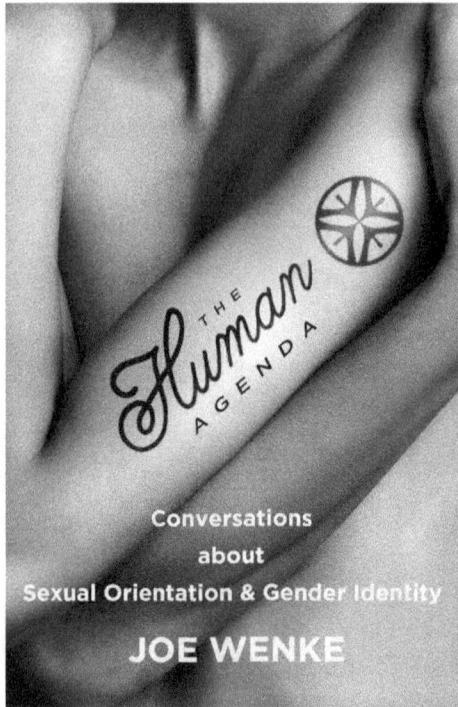

JOE WENKE'S THE HUMAN AGENDA

In THE HUMAN AGENDA: Conversations About Sexual Orientation & Gender Identity, LGBTQI advocate Joe Wenke speaks with some of the community's leading change agents. In these wide-ranging and probing conversations, amazing people share their personal and professional stories along with their profound commitment to freedom and equality.

GISELE ALICEA, (aka GISELE XTRAVAGANZA) *fashion model:* "Transgender people are real people. We have mothers. We have fathers. . . . We have families. We have somewhere that we came from."

ASH BECKHAM, *speaker and advocate:* "It's really hard to not empathize with someone that you have a human connection with."

IAN HARVIE, *comedian:* "It is brave to be yourself."

DR. CARYS MASSARELLA, *emergency physician:* "Being transgender is not biologically hazardous."

CARMEN CARRERA, *performer and fashion model:* "We are one human race. Some women have penises. Some men have vaginas. What's the big deal?"

ELEGANCE BRATTON, *filmmaker:* "There is such a massive gap in understanding between what has been sold as the gay life and what has been the experience of gay people of color."

ANDRE ST. CLAIR, *actor:* "You can refer to me as male or female. As long as you're not doing it disrespectfully, I'll respond."

Y-LOVE, *hip hop artist:* "You can only have unity through diversity. Otherwise, it's just homogeneity."

ANDREW SOLOMON, *author:* "I think there is a tyranny of the norm. . . . But actually what science indicates is that diversity is what strengthens a society or a culture or a species."

Also featuring Kristin Russo, Aidan Key, Hida Viloria, Hina Wong-Kalu, Dr. Jonipher Kupono-Kwong and other leading change agents.

THE HUMAN AGENDA addresses some of the most critical issues facing the LGBTQI community, including:

- The marginalization of transgender people

- Breaking down the sexual orientation and gender identity binaries

- The fluidity of sexual orientation and gender identity

- The challenges of coming out

- The religious justification for bigotry against LGBTQI people

- Marriage equality

- The right to adopt children

- The politics of difference: sexual orientation, gender identity and race

- Reclaiming language: the power of "queer"

JOE WENKE'S THE TALK SHOW, A NOVEL

Someone is following Jack Winthrop—most likely the gunman who tried to kill America's most controversial talk show host, Abraham Lincoln Jones. Ever since that fateful night when Jones called Winthrop with his audacious proposal, life has never been the same. Winthrop, an award-winning New York Times reporter who calls the Tit for Tat strip club his second home, agreed to collaborate on Jones' national "Emancipation Tour." The plan is to bring Jones' passion for radical change to the people and transcend television by meeting America face to face. Now Winthrop has to survive long enough to make the tour a reality.

As the reach of his stalker spreads, so does the fear that Winthrop's unconventional family is also in danger—Rita Harvey, the gentle transgender ex-priest and LGBT activist; Slow Mo, the massive vegetarian bouncer; and Donna, stripper and entrepreneurial prodigy—as well as the woman who is claiming his heart, media expert Danielle Jackson.

Steeped in the seamy underbelly of New York City, THE TALK SHOW is a fast-paced and mordantly funny thriller that examines how the forces of nihilism threaten our yearning for love, family and acceptance.

JOE WENKE ON FREE AIR

"The poems are very entertaining. Each one is like a little surprise package for the reader to open up. If you enjoy experiencing little epiphanies and revelations about a variety of subjects, including freedom, equality, mortality, troubled relationships, human identity, love and the mysteries of existence, then these poems are for you."

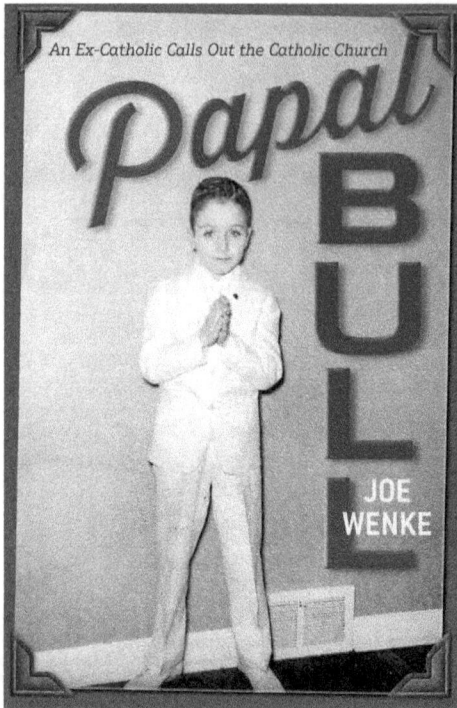

An Ex-Catholic Calls Out the Catholic Church

Papal BULL

JOE WENKE

PRAISE FOR JOE WENKE'S PAPAL BULL

"I may burn in hell for even having read this book."
John C. Wood

"If you enjoyed Wenke's take on the Bible, *You Got to Be Kidding!* read his exegesis of the Catholic Church's past two thousand years. . . . Mordantly funny, scrupulously researched."
E. B. Boatner, Lavender Magazine

"If you wonder why a 'merciful' God created a no-exit-ever hell or if you entertain thoughts of how boring the traditional religious notion of heaven might be, you will meet a savagely witty ally in Wenke's book." *Joe Meyers, CTPost*

"I absolutely LOVED this book. . . . I highly recommend it to any Catholic who is considering recovering from his condition." *Philip G. Harding*

"Joe Wenke is an extraordinary writer. . . . This book is an enlightening journey (for both the author and the reader) that was tenderly written by an exceptional person who is not afraid to let others know about what occurs in so many families, causing a great deal of pain and uncertainty. It is something that should be read by anyone and everyone, regardless of their religion or how they were raised/told by others to believe. There are no words to express the depth of my gratitude to Mr. Wenke and I will be anxiously awaiting any other material that he wishes to write, because I am a lifelong fan." *Jules*

"Ex-Catholics will love this book. It is an amazing satire of the Catholic Church. Every bit as funny as *You Got To Be Kidding!* I highly recommend." *Holly Michele*

"I love this book! It is not only informative but funny as hell." *Rick Martin*

"Funny, clever and spot on." *V. Kennedy*

"Whew! I feel like I've been to confession with the universe, (not God, that's a bad fairytale) and I've been absolved of . . . something. Thank you, Dr. Wenke, for putting into words . . . what I've been thinking about religion, especially Catholicism for a long time. . . . The one thought that kept repeating for me throughout the book, was that I need to buy about 2 dozen copies of this and hand them out to my family members, and at least try to spark a conversation." *Deborah*

"Papal Bull is brilliant and funny, well-researched and informative. . . . [Wenke] writes with humor that is at once scathing, insightful and absurd. His recounting of stories from Catholic grade school made me laugh out loud." *Lori Giampa*

"A cutting, satirical look at Catholic beliefs regarding saints, Mary, birth control, the treatment of women, and of course the huge scandalous cover-up of molestation." *Tiffany A. Harkleroad*

"Impeccably researched and sharply written. . . . [Wenke's] wit and incisive perspective consistently deliver humor and important points to anyone willing to open their minds. . . . A work in which you can think, laugh, and ask the important questions is a must-read." *David Nor*

"For some reason, I kept falling into a George Carlin voice as I read the book." *Joseph Spuckler*

"I love the cover and I love the term 'recovering Catholic' of which I believe I am one. I think any one who went to Catholic School in the fifties and sixties . . . probably had many of the same experiences that the author describes from his school years." *Diane Scholl*

A great and sometimes funny book all 'recovering Catholics' should read. In fact it should be required reading for anybody who considers themselves Holy. Brilliant insight & questions every Catholic should ask themselves." *Robert Kennemer*

"It is necessary to call the church out on their horrendous errors and this book is much needed in society. . . . *Papal Bull* is timely and makes for some very interesting reading. Enjoy!" *Lynda Smock*

"I not only laughed a great deal, but [the book] also gave me a lot to think about." *Michele Barbrow*

"A must read. Excellent!" *Carole*

"This satirical book mocks the church by using actual historical facts. It is a critical and at times humorous analysis of the church's history from a modern perspective." *Katarina Nolte*

"This was a wild ride. I found parts to be rather upsetting but I think the author really did his homework." *Sher Brown*

"An incredibly clever and humorous take on the Catholic Church." *ChristophFischerBooks*

"Wonderfully sacrilegious." *Joe R. Mcauley*

"I absolutely LOVED this book. . . . I highly recommend it to any Catholic who is considering recovering from his condition, and definitely to any atheist, agnostic, or humanist who wants to get the "inside drum" on these religious nutters." *Philip G. Harding*

"A great . . . book all "recovering Catholics" should read. In fact it should be required reading for anybody who considers themselves Holy. Brilliant insight & questions every Catholic should ask themselves." *Robert Kennemer*

"This was a great book. . . . infused with humor and biting wit. It is also a great expose of Catholicism and its many irrationalities and absurdities. As a fellow ex-Catholic who also enjoys calling out the Catholic Church, I can't recommend this book enough." *Alexander*

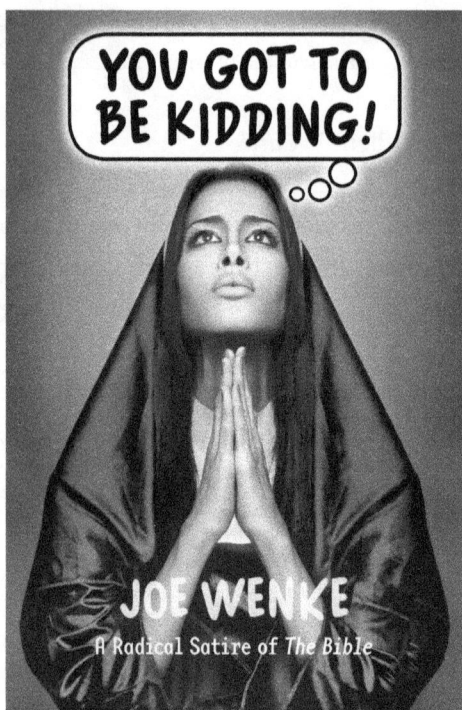

"This is hilarious! Joe Wenke gives a nod to Mark Twain as he looks at the Bible with fresh eyes and with the pen of a thinking comic." *Bill Baker*

"This is without a doubt the funniest book I've ever read. I sat with my parents and read aloud some of the passages and we all laughed a lot!" *Emma Charlton, Bookswithemma*

"Very tongue-in-cheek, sarcastic and pointed, dedicated to Christopher Hitchens and Thomas Paine, both of whom would, I believe, really enjoy this book!" *Sarah Hulcey*

"The cover of the book itself is a slap in the face of transphobia. . . . If this book accomplishes one thing, I hope it pushes prejudiced people toward acceptance of LGBT people just as they are." *Isaac James Baker, Reading, Writing & Wine*

"Brave, brilliant and funny. Page after page, biblical chapter after biblical chapter, absurdity after absurdity, this book delivers laugh after laugh. Joe Wenke has crafted the answer to the fundamentalist literal reading of the Bible with the perfect recipe of rationality, candor and humor." *Max Gelt*

"Brilliant . . . for once a funny look at ALL the Bible's insanity." *Jo Bryant*

"Would make a really wicked Christmas present for your Christian friends who have a sense of humor and a sense of the ridiculous." *Ed Buckner, American Atheists*

"Oh my! This is very funny . . . Joe turns everything on its head and makes it a really interesting read." *Stephen Ormsby*

"BEST THING I've READ IN AGES" *Phillip A. Reeves*

"Whether you are an atheist or a Christian who can see the absurdity of some of the anecdotes narrated in Holy Scripture, Joe Wenke's humor won't be wasted on you." *Mina's Bookshelf*

"Great book! Funny and easy to read." *Violets and Tulips*

"Funny and to the point read. Takes a look at the Bible and points out all sorts of inaccuracies, illogical stories and questions. Strongly recommend." *Hertzey*

"Witty and wise. Joe Wenke takes a critical, provocative look at The Bible and he does so with regular hilarity." *Dana Hislop*

"A must-read for anyone who still thinks the Bible is the inviolable word of God—sense of humor mandatory." *K. Sozaeva*

"Such a funny read, my son & I actually read it together! Laughter abounds!" *Rael*

"Deliciously witty!" *Jack Scott*

"Irreverent and hilarious. I am no Bible scholar, but I feel like I have been given the funniest crib notes on this most widely read and probably as widely misunderstood book of all time. I laughed out loud at Wenke's common sense observations and interpretations of this tome." *Lorna Lee*

"Will keep any freethinking reader laughing the whole way through." *George Lichman*

"[*You Got to Be Kidding* is] entertaining and enlightening."
Patti Bray

"You will be laughing yourself silly while reading this book! In fact, you may find yourself bookmarking a bunch of pages to discuss with your pastor and friends later!" *S. Henke*

"I could not put this book down." *Jackie Hepton*

"This author allows the reader to explore and learn about the Bible with a tongue-in-cheek attitude that keeps you laughing and turning the pages." *Tricia Schneider*

"Some of it made me feel like I might wind up in hell for reading it, but if you keep an open mind and a light heart, you'll have a blast." *Jon Yost*

"Don't read the Bible! Read this!" *Dr. Dan*

"I'm still laughing." *Paul Wilson*

"GREAT. What hogwash we have been fed. Thanks, Joe." *Colin M. Maybury*

"Unforgiving and hilarious." *Phil*

"This book is so funny." *Crystal*

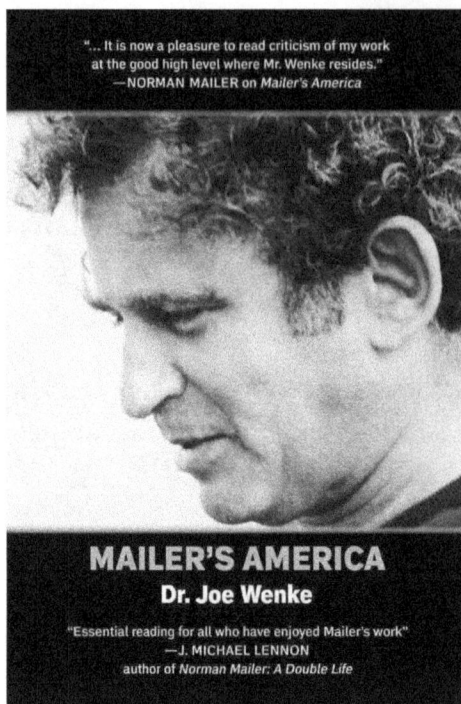

"... It is now a pleasure to read criticism of my work at the good high level where Mr. Wenke resides."
—NORMAN MAILER on *Mailer's America*

MAILER'S AMERICA
Dr. Joe Wenke

"Essential reading for all who have enjoyed Mailer's work"
—J. MICHAEL LENNON
author of *Norman Mailer: A Double Life*

PRAISE FOR JOE WENKE'S MAILER'S AMERICA

The reissue of Joseph Wenke's thoughtful study, *Mailer's America*, provides renewed hope for a deeper understanding of Mailer's work. No other commentator has focused so relentlessly on the deepest purpose of Mailer's hugely varied oeuvre, namely to "clarify a nation's vision of itself." Wenke's examination inhabits, patrols and maps the territory between the millennial promise of America and its often dispiriting actuality. His study contains probing, nuanced and careful examinations of all Mailer's work though the mid-1980s, including one of the first major examinations of Mailer's most demanding novel, *Ancient Evenings*. Wenke's book deserves a wide audience, and is essential reading for all who have enjoyed Mailer's work.—*J. Michael Lennon, author of the authorized biography, Norman Mailer: A Double Life*

www.ingramcontent.com/pod-product-compliance
Lightning Source LLC
Chambersburg PA
CBHW020515030426
42337CB00011B/392